AF261226
FOREST PATTERN
12 SHEETS SINGLE-SIDED
SCRAPBOOKING DESIGNS FOR CRAFTS
SCRAPBOOK PAPER PAD
6x6, NON-PERFORATED SHEETS
© Crafty As Ever

To remove cut along the dotted line.

TO REMOVE CUT ALONG THE DOTTED LINE.

To remove cut along the dotted line.